First American edition 1998 by
Franklin Watts
A Division of Grolier Publishing
Sherman Turnpike
Danbury, CT 06816

ISBN 0-513-14494-1 (lib. bdg.)        0-531-15353-3 (pbk.)

A copy of the Cataloging-in-Publication Data is available from the Library of
Congress

Printed in Belgium

Editor: Samantha Armstrong
Art Director: Robert Walster
Designer: Diane Thistlethwaite
Illustrator: Teri Gower
Consultant: John Illingworth, Consultant in
Construction Methods and Technology

Picture credits: Chris Fairclough 10; Image Bank 7; J C Bamford Excavators Ltd.
16-17; QA Photo Library cover, 6, 15, 22-23, 24-25; Robert Harding 8-9, 26; John
Walmsley Photography 12; Scott Wilson 18; Zefa 13, 21.

# MACHINES AT WORK

# Building a
# Road

FRANKLIN WATTS
A Division of Grolier Publishing
NEW YORK • LONDON • HONG KONG • SYDNEY
DANBURY, CONNECTICUT

Roads are everywhere.
We use different machines
to build and repair them.

Before a new road
can be built, the ground
has to be made flat.

Giant excavators dig, cut, and move the soil for the new road.

They also make room for drains
along the side of the road.
When the road is finished,
rain will run off the road
into the drains.

Excavators run on
Caterpillar tracks
to help them move
over rough ground
without getting stuck.

A spreader is used to move
the soil over the ground
so that it is level.

Dump trucks carry away
any unwanted soil.

Next a soil compactor
moves slowly over the ground
to make it hard and flat.

The soil compactor's
heavy roller has bumps
on it which help to
push down the soil.

A front-end loader collects
a mixture of crushed stones
and takes it to the site.

Hydraulic pumps help
the front-end loader
to lift heavy loads.

20

409B

This mixture forms the base,
or foundation, of the road.

Graders scrape along
the foundation to make
the surface smooth.

Graders make sure
the whole road
is the same level.

A top surface is laid over
the foundation. This can be
made of concrete or asphalt (tar).
It provides a waterproof and
long-lasting road.

Hot asphalt is
dumped slowly out of
the dump truck.

Asphalt is spread while it is hot.
It is very sticky!

# A heavy road roller
# flattens the hot asphalt.

The roller
goes slowly
over the
soft asphalt.

Sometimes bridges are built
so that roads can cross
each other, a river,
or a railway.

After a time, traffic wears out the surface of the road.

Often jackhammers
and other small machines
are used to make repairs.

Even small machines,
like this jackhammer, can
be very noisy!

Earmuffs protect
the driller's ears
against damage
from the noise.

# Glossary

**Bulldozers** are heavy tractors with blades at the front to push and spread earth.

**Dump trucks** move different materials from one place to another.

jackhammer

**Excavators** dig and move earth.

**Front-end loaders** use their buckets to lift earth or stones.

**Graders** carefully level the foundation of the road.

roller

**Jackhammers** dig up old or worn out asphalt.

**Rollers** smooth and flatten the earth.

**Soil compactors** move over the earth and make it flat.

soil compactor

# Index

dump truck

grader